YLVA HILLSTRÖM
& KARIN EKLUND

# THE ART AND LIFE OF
# HILMA AF KLINT

T&H

In late October 1862, when the sun was in the sign of Scorpio, a little girl was born at Karlberg Palace in Stockholm, Sweden. She was named Hilma af Klint. According to the positions of the stars and planets on the day that she was born, Hilma's life would be filled with magic and mystery.

Several generations of the af Klint family were commanders in the Navy and drew nautical charts. These charts mapped what lay beneath the sea along Sweden's coasts, so that ships could stay safe. One day, Hilma would also draw maps of what couldn't be seen, but not maps of what's hidden under water. Hers would be maps of the spirit world.

Sometimes Hilma thought she could hear things that other people couldn't hear and see things that other people couldn't see. Not exactly ghosts, but something similar. Now and then, she felt like she knew what was going to happen, long before it actually did.

In the summer, the af Klint family lived on the island of Adelsö in Lake Mälaren. Hilma, her younger sister Hermina, and their sisters and brother learned math, sailing, physics, and botany. It was fun, but more than anything else, Hilma loved drawing. She drew pictures of almost all the flowers she saw.

"Look at this, Hilma," said her father one day. "It's a magic square. Study it carefully and tell me what's magical about it."

Hilma thought so hard that her brain almost tingled.

"Goodness me," her father said as he read the newspaper. "It says here that a Scotsman named Alexander Graham Bell has invented something called a telephone. It's a device you can use to talk to someone even if you're in different parts of the world. It sounds like magic!"

"Papa!" Hilma said, waving her hand excitedly in the air. "I've figured out exactly how the magic square works!"*

* In a magic square, the numbers in each column and each row add up to the same total. The numbers in the corners of the square also add up to the same total.

In the 19th and early 20th century, there were lots of discoveries that showed that the world is filled with invisible waves.

In 1837, **Samuel Morse** and his colleagues invented the electric telegraph. They turned the alphabet into a code made up of dots and dashes. This Morse code could be used to send messages over long distances.

In 1876, **Alexander Graham Bell** patented the telephone.

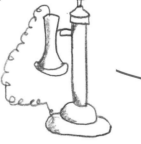

In 1879, **Thomas Edison** launched his version of the electric light bulb.

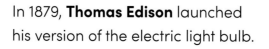

In 1885–89, **Heinrich Hertz** proved that light and heat are made from electromagnetic waves.

In 1895, **Wilhelm Conrad Röntgen** discovered X-rays. These let doctors see inside the human body without cutting it open.

In 1905, **Albert Einstein** showed that the world is made up of tiny, invisible particles, called atoms.

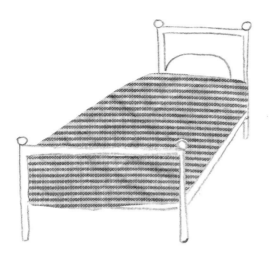

A few days before Hilma turned eighteen, something terrible happened. Her little sister Hermina, who was just ten years old, fell ill and died.

One evening not long afterward, Hilma was sitting alone in her room, drawing. It was very quiet. The only sound that could be heard was the rasping of her pen on the paper. Then something made her stop. The flame of her candle flickered. Hilma looked behind her, but saw nothing.

"Hilma?"

There seemed to be a soft voice coming out of thin air.

Hilma's blood ran cold.

"Who's there?" Hilma asked.

"It's me. Hermina!"

Hilma's fear melted away. To her surprise, it didn't feel strange to be talking to Hermina, even though her sister was dead. It felt as though she was close by, perhaps standing behind a curtain.

A couple of years after Hermina's death, Hilma began studying art at the Royal Swedish Academy of Fine Arts in Stockholm.

How wonderful it was to draw and paint all day long! The studios at the school smelled of turpentine and oil paint—artists' smells.

Light streamed in through the big windows in the room where drawing classes were held. There were only women in Hilma's class. In fact, women being able to study at the Academy was quite new. Not long before, only men were allowed to go there.

"Women shouldn't be allowed to paint at all," a male student said to one of the professors.

Hilma and her best friend Anna looked at one another and shook their heads. What a silly thing to say!

When Hilma finished her studies, she found a studio in the middle of Stockholm. She painted landscapes and sometimes people asked her to paint their portrait. Her paintings of flowers were very realistic, almost like photographs.

*Botanical Study*, 1890s

In America, the sisters **Kate and Maggie Fox** claimed that they could receive messages from the dead. They became world-famous. Spiritualism—the belief that it is possible to speak to the dead—grew very popular in America and Europe in the mid-19th century.

The Fox sisters received messages from the dead in the form of a series of tapping sounds, some long and some short, a little like Morse code.

Years later, it was discovered that the Fox sisters had lied. The sounds didn't come from the spirit world at all, but from Kate and Maggie cracking their toe and knee joints. But spiritualism still remained popular and it was fashionable to hold seances, where groups of people would gather to try to contact the spirit world.

The ability to contact the spirit world
was something that followed Hilma
into adulthood. She and Anna decided
to explore the invisible world together.

Their friends Mathilda, Cornelia,
and Sigrid wanted to join in too. They
formed a kind of secret society called
The Five. They thought the name
sounded mysterious.

The Five lit candles on an altar and prayed together, as if they were in church. Then Sigrid lay down on the sofa and concentrated so deeply that she fell into a trance.

At first nothing happened, but then it was as if she had managed to tune into the right channel. A voice filled the room.

I AM GREGOR

It was Sigrid speaking, but her voice sounded much deeper than usual. Hilma got goose bumps. They were talking to a spirit!

While Sigrid was in a trance, she passed on messages from Gregor and several other spirits. The Five took turns writing down what she said. Sometimes the messages came in the form of pictures and then it was almost always Cornelia who took control of the pen. Hilma thought this wasn't fair. She was an artist, after all. Why shouldn't she draw for the spirits too?

Hilma wondered why the spirits never gave her any important
messages. Didn't she know enough about the spirit world?
Perhaps she could change that.

"Why are you sitting there, staring at that glass of water?"
Anna asked one afternoon.

"I'm practicing," Hilma replied.

"Practicing what?"

"My spiritual abilities. There's a secret in the water.
If I look at it long enough, I will understand."

Hilma stretched. She was stubborn and patient, but her neck was stiff and her legs ached. Staring at a glass of water for hours was boring. It also made her thirsty.

What is water, really? Molecules composed of the tiniest particles—atoms. Two hydrogen atoms and one oxygen atom. Water has existed since the beginning of time, and is essential to life on Earth.

Hilma looked at the glass again. Perhaps a dinosaur once drank these very molecules. Or a seahorse swam around in them. Water is something eternal. She smiled to herself, as though she had suddenly understood something important.

Then she drank the water and went out to get some air.

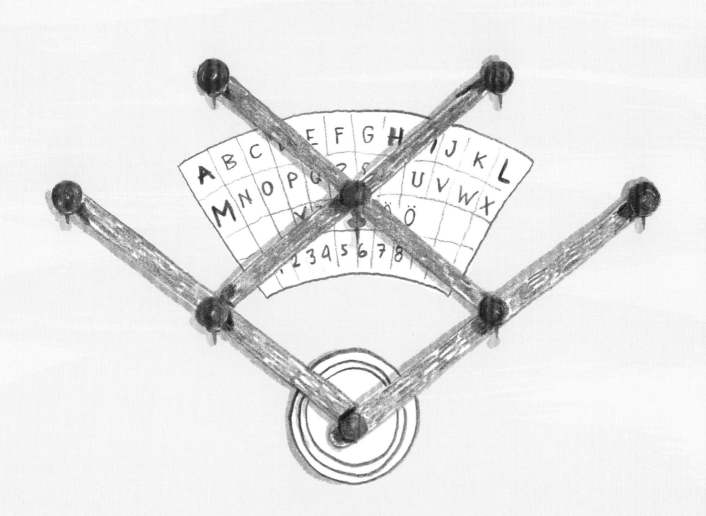

Sometimes The Five used a spirit board to make contact with the spirits. A spirit board was a piece of cardboard with the letters of the alphabet written on it and a special wooden pointer called a planchette. Mathilda lightly held the planchette, and asked the spirits a question.

The planchette would suddenly begin to slide over the letters. Then it stopped. After a moment, it moved again, and then stopped once more. The Five wrote down all the letters it stopped at. The letters they collected formed words and sentences.

One evening, they made contact with a spirit who called himself Amaliel. He said that one of The Five would be given a special task to do—making paintings of the invisible world of the spirits.

The tension in the room was high, and Hilma could hear her heart pounding in her chest. Then the pointer began to move. It felt like an eternity before it stopped at the first letter: H …

This is soon followed by an I …

Then L … M … A.

At last, Hilma had been given a job to do!

Hilma agreed to take on the task without knowing how it would work. The idea of painting pictures that contained messages from the universe was more than she'd ever dreamed of! Happiness, hope, and fear swirled inside her. How would she do it?

To prepare herself, she decided not to paint anything at all for a few months, no portraits and no landscapes. She meditated and was careful about what she ate. No meat and absolutely no fish or seafood. She wanted to keep her mind and body clean and healthy.

*Primordial Chaos, No. 16*, 1906–7

At last, the time came. Hilma threw herself into the unknown and got started. She felt free, now that none of her paintings had to look like the real world. Her paintbrushes could dance across the canvas however they wanted.

The spirits told her which signs and symbols to paint. Triangles and circles, crosses and spirals, roses and lilies flowed onto the canvas. Letters that didn't form words. Puzzles and riddles made of colors and shapes. But what did it all mean? Even Hilma herself didn't know.

*The Ten Largest, No. 2, Childhood,* 1907

*The Ten Largest, No. 3, Youth*, 1907

When Hilma finished painting for the day, she cut off contact with the invisible world. She spent the rest of her time doing ordinary, everyday things, like buying eggs. It took lots of eggs to make the paint she used. Hundreds, in fact!

Hilma af Klint
and many other artists and
authors in the early 20th century
were interested in a way of thinking called
**theosophy**. Theosophists believe that all the
religions in the world come from
the same spiritual tradition. They
also think that there is a spark
of the divine in all living beings.
Helena Petrovna Blavatsky
founded the Theosophical
Society in New York in 1875.

THE SECRET DOCTRINE

By 1908, Hilma had spent more than a year painting pictures. One day, she found out that the famous author and theosophist Rudolf Steiner was coming to Stockholm. She had read several of his books and wanted to show him her paintings, so she wrote to him and invited him to visit her in her studio.

But when Steiner arrived, he looked around in silence and shook his head. He thought it was strange that spirits could have painted pictures through her brushes. He told her she ought to spend her time reading and studying instead. Then he yawned. Hilma could hardly believe it. She had shown him paintings that contained messages from the universe to humanity! How could he be bored by that? She couldn't understand it.

"Goodbye, Miss af Klint." Steiner left her studio without saying another word.

"But…" she started, then fell silent. What can you say to someone who doesn't want to listen?

After Rudolf Steiner went back to Germany, Hilma stopped painting. No one understood what she was doing. At least, that's how it felt.

Steiner often gave lectures about spiritual and mystical subjects. Lots of people wanted to see and hear him. One of the people who came to listen was Wassily Kandinsky. He was an artist, just like Hilma.

"Mr. Steiner," said Kandinsky, "I am trying to come up with something new. Something no one has painted before. Paintings that say something about the universe."

"I see," said Steiner. "Well, I have something to tell you, Mr. Kandinsky." Then Steiner whispered something into Kandinsky's ear.

At home in Sweden, Hilma studied different religions and myths. Many of the stories she read were about people going on adventures to unknown places.

The heroes of the stories often faced obstacles, fought monsters, and explored the underworld. Then they came back home with new knowledge. She read about knights searching for the Holy Grail and about alchemists hunting for the Philosopher's Stone. All of these stories were about people looking for answers to life's big questions.

The Five no longer spent much time together and they stopped holding seances. But Anna often visited Hilma.

"Here's something interesting," Hilma said one afternoon. "Everything on earth has an equivalent in the universe. Atoms look like little planets. The spiral shapes of galaxies are the same as the shape of a tiny snail's shell. Even the branches and the roots of a tree look the same."

*The Seven-Pointed Star, No. 2,* 1908

Hilma named one series of paintings *The Seven-Pointed Star,* even though there were no stars with seven points in any of them. She wondered if the world would ever see her paintings. In the meantime, they gathered dust in her studio.

**Alchemy** is an ancient science that came before modern chemistry. The aim of alchemy was to transform one material into another material that was more noble and more perfect. Many alchemists dreamed of turning other metals into gold, but they also believed that the soul could be made pure, and brought closer to the divine.

It was said that the famous alchemist, **Nicolas Flamel**, who lived in Paris in the 14th century with his wife Perenelle, managed to create a Philosopher's Stone. According to alchemists, this stone was a legendary object that could turn metals into gold or give humans eternal life. The house where the Flamels lived in Paris is still standing today.

One day, Hilma met up with Anna to have tea.
"Look at this!" she said.

Hilma held up a pine cone and counted the spirals
made by the spikes. Five in one direction, eight in the
other. She counted the spirals in the middle of a flower.
Thirteen in one direction, twenty-one in the other.

"The plants' seeds and petals grow in spiral shapes,"
she said. "The number of spirals is almost always a
number from a list called the Fibonacci sequence.
Each number in the sequence is the sum of the two
numbers before it: 1, 1, 2, 3, 5, 8, 13, 21, 34, 55…"

Anna looked doubtful. "Try counting the spirals
in this sunflower," she said. "There are lots of them!"

Hilma marked the sunflower seeds with paint to
make them easier to count. Yellow in one direction,
blue in the other.

"34 and 55! You see? It's almost like magic."
Then she laughed.

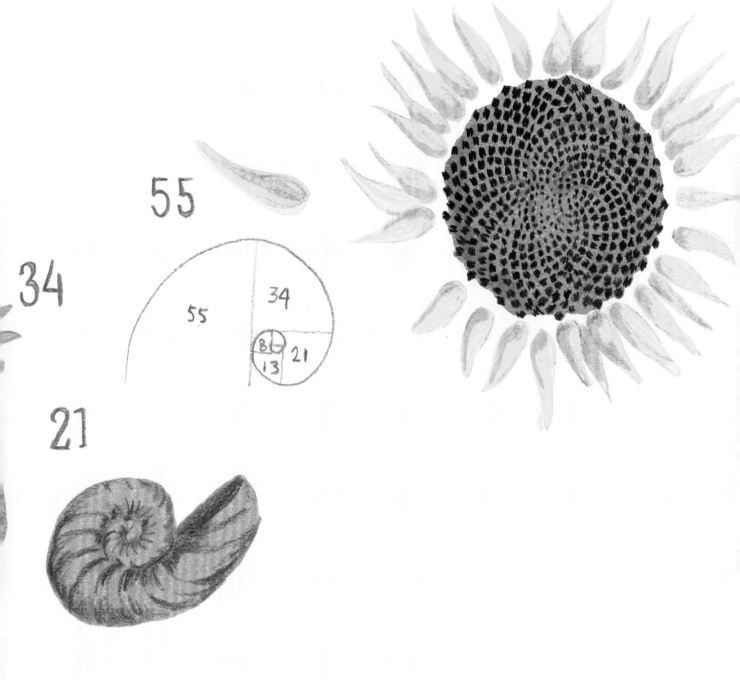

"What's so funny?" Anna asked.

Hilma put her teacup on the table. "I was thinking about how scientists like to put everything into categories. They want to control life itself. At the same time, we humans are helplessly whirling around together on a small planet, floating in space, which is infinitely huge. And there's nothing we can do about it, no matter how much we count, measure, and weigh."

In Germany, Wassily Kandinsky kept painting. Like Hilma, he tried to create pictures of the spiritual side of life. Paintings in deep blue, ruby red, and emerald green.

Kandinsky had a special ability called synesthesia. This is when the senses combine together in unusual ways. It meant he could hear how colors sound and see colors in music. To him, paintings were like symphonies made up of colors and shapes.

The very first abstract painting in the world was created in 1911 by me. No other painter created abstract pictures at this time.

Best wishes,

KANDINSKY.

K

"This is amazing!" said admirers of art. "Kandinsky has invented the first abstract art!"

No one had heard of the Swedish artist Hilma af Klint, even though she had made abstract paintings several years before Kandinsky did. But Hilma didn't care. She never painted to be famous. Instead, she wanted to understand the universe.

*Altarpiece, No. 1*, 1915

## SYMBOLS AND WHAT THEY MEAN

A symbol can mean different things, depending on where and how it's used. Some of these explanations are the ones that Hilma herself wrote down, while others are more general.

**Shell** – spiritual growth.

**Ouroboros** (a snake or dragon swallowing its own tail) – unity, or the union of opposites.

**Triangle** – the Holy Trinity, or salt, sulphur and lead.

**Triangle with its point upwards** – the sign for man, or growth.

**Triangle with its point downwards** – the sign for woman, or the Holy Grail.

**The Holy Grail** – the chalice that Jesus drank from during the Last Supper, or a way of depicting the Philosopher's Stone.

**The Philosopher's Stone** – a legendary object that can be used to make gold.

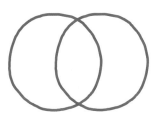

**Vesica Piscis** (an almond-like shape formed when two circles overlap) – the Holy Grail, or the union of opposites.

**Blue** – the female principle.

**Yellow** – the male principle.

**Gold** – perfection, the sun or God.

**Silver** – the moon.

**Infinity sign** (a sideways figure eight) – infinity.

**Rose** – the male principle.

**Lily** – the female principle.

**Swan** – the spiritual, or the union of opposites.

**The Seven-Pointed Star** – the divine, or creation itself.

After a break of nearly four years, Hilma felt ready to pick up her paints and brushes again to finish the task that the spirit Amaliel had given her. She no longer allowed the spirits to control her brushes, but she still painted their messages.

*The Swan, No. 1,* 1915

*The Swan, No. 8,* 1915

When Hilma finished her *Altarpiece* series, her
task was complete and she could relax. The three
large *Altarpiece* paintings seemed to sum up the
work she was trying to do. The rainbow ladder
looks like it leads up to a golden sun, while
the dark one seems to go down to the
underworld. After the last painting, the
one with the big circle, was done,
she had painted 193 pictures.

All these paintings would
look good inside a temple,
she thought. A spiral-shaped
building that looked like
a seashell or a galaxy.

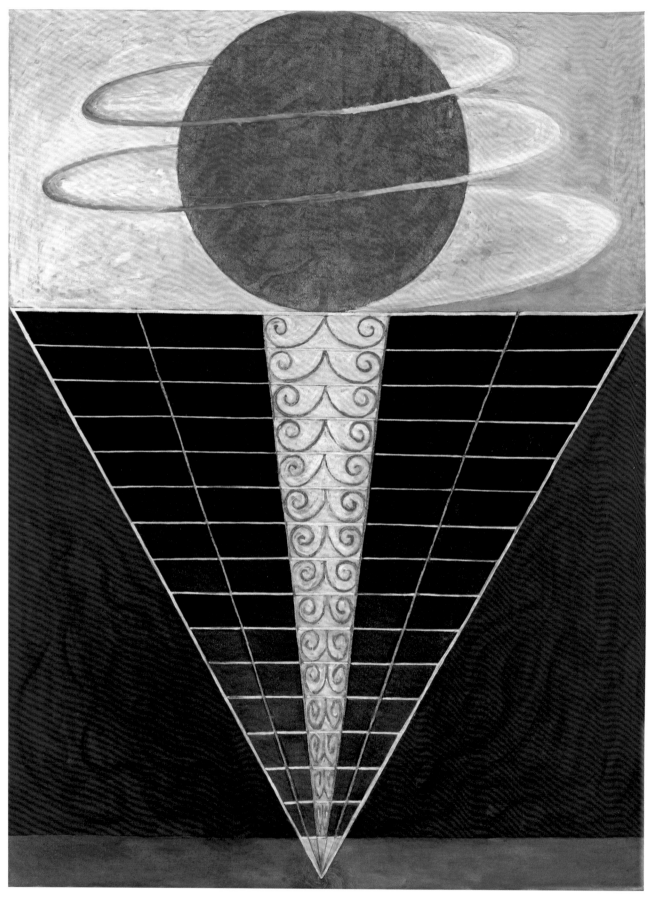

*Altarpiece, No. 2*, 1915

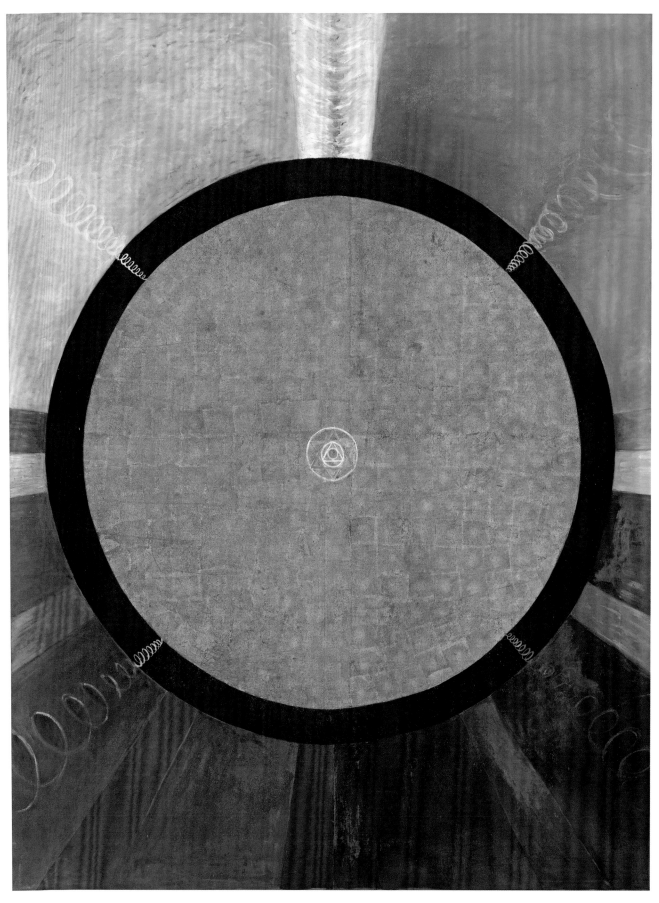

*Altarpiece, No. 3*, 1915

She made many series
of paintings, exploring
different subjects.
One series was called
*The Swan*. Some of
the paintings in the
series show a black
swan and a white
swan, but some of the
others don't contain
anything realistic
at all. Perhaps they
are images of the
swan's soul.

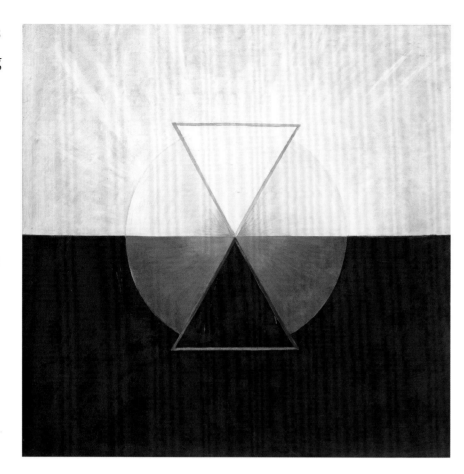

*The Swan, No. 13,* 1915

*The Swan, No. 24,* 1915

Over the years that followed, Hilma continued to paint abstract pictures. She made paintings that depict small things and big things, atoms and religions.

She made her pictures from the basic shapes that her father taught her about when she was little. Circles, squares, triangles and rectangles.

Hilma also filled many notebooks with her thoughts about the invisible world. The pages were bursting with lists and explanations of various signs and symbols.

*Series V, No. 4*, 1920

Hilma took the train to Switzerland
several times to hear Rudolf Steiner
giving lectures. He had designed a
building he called the Goetheanum.
People came from all over to
study spiritual matters there.

   She had an idea. What
if the Goetheanum was
the temple where her
paintings belonged?

Hilma thought that the whole world should share the messages in her pictures and that Steiner could help her. She was afraid that without his help, her artworks might be forgotten for ever.

"Mr Steiner. I want to donate my paintings to the Goetheanum. Will you accept them?"

"Hmm…" Steiner looked out the window. "Look at that beautiful eagle flying out there," he said, and walked away.

Hilma was sad and shocked. He didn't want her paintings. She thought about destroying them all. But instead she went home and kept doing the thing she loved most—painting.

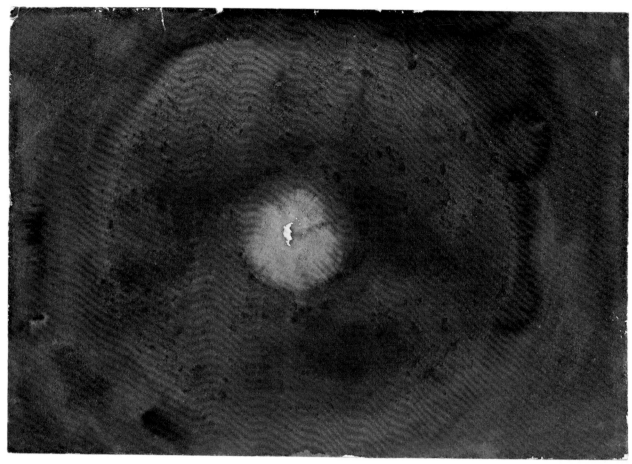

*The Birch Tree,* 1922

The paintings she made next were different. She started painting with watercolors, sometimes on wet paper. The colors flowed around the paper and mixed together. Instead of painting realistic images of plants, she let the colors show their innermost selves, as though flowers and trees also had secrets.

*Untitled*, 1924

Years went by. In Europe, World War II was raging. Hilma was over eighty years old and knew that her time on earth would soon come to an end. She had painted more than a thousand pictures but almost no one had seen them.

Hilma's nephew Erik af Klint was a vice-admiral in the Swedish Navy. One day, his aunt asked him to come for a visit. She had something important to ask him.

"Erik, I want you to take care of my paintings," she said. "No one must see them until I've been dead for twenty years."

Although she was old, her posture was still straight and her gaze was steely and determined.

"But dear aunt, why?" Erik asked.

"The time isn't right yet," she said.

"But what on earth do all these paintings mean?" he asked.

"I don't actually know," Hilma replied.

When Hilma
died in 1944,
Erik put all the crates
filled with her works of art
and notebooks in his attic. In the
winter, it was freezing cold up there,
and in the summer, it was blazing hot.
Paintings need a constant temperature, or they
can be damaged. But Erik had other things to think
about, besides his aunt's paintings.

More than twenty years passed before he went up to the attic
again. It was dark there and full of cobwebs, and a musty smell
tickled his nose. Before he opened the first crate, he paused,
wondering what he might find. Her paintings were
rolled up and packed inside like sardines.

One at a time, he unrolled them.
Unbelievably, they had survived.
What a relief! It was finally time
for the world to see them.

Several decades have passed since those crates in the attic were first opened. Now, hundreds of thousands of people visit museums around the world to see Hilma's paintings. No one has ever seen anything like them, and everyone is amazed. With these paintings as a map, anyone who wants to can take a journey to unknown places, just like the sailors in the af Klint family and the heroes from the myths and stories that Hilma loved.

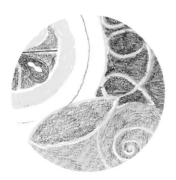

But if Hilma's paintings are maps, what do they show and how should we read them?

There's no easy answer to this question. The right way to read a map changes, depending on the position of the person reading it.

And that's something that everybody has to work out for themselves.

Ylva Hillström has also published two books about art in Swedish:
*KONST – titta, upptäck, gör* and *SKAPA tillsammans med barnen*.

List of works by Hilma af Klint featured in this book:
*Botanical Study*, 1890s
*The WU/Rose series, Group I, Primordial Chaos, No. 16*, 1906–7
*Untitled Series, Group IV, The Ten Largest, No. 2, Childhood*, 1907
*Untitled Series, Group IV, The Ten Largest, No. 3, Youth*, 1907
*The WUS/Seven-Pointed Star Series, Group V, The Seven-Pointed Star, No. 2*, 1908
*The SUW Series, Group IX, The Swan, No. 1*, 1915
*The SUW Series, Group IX, The Swan, No. 8*, 1915
*The SUW Series, Group IX, The Swan, No. 13*, 1915
*The SUW Series, Group IX, The Swan, No. 24*, 1915
*Untitled series, Group X, Altarpiece, No. 1*, 1915
*Untitled series, Group X, Altarpiece, No. 2*, 1915
*Untitled series, Group X, Altarpiece, No. 3*, 1915
*Series V, No. 4*, 1920
*On the Viewing of Flowers and Trees, The Birch*, 1922
*Untitled*, 1924

Thanks to the Hilma af Klint Foundation: www.hilmaafklint.se

Translated from the Swedish by B.J. Epstein

First published in the United Kingdom in 2022 by
Thames & Hudson Ltd, 181A High Holborn, London WC1V 7QX

First published in the United States of America in 2022 by
Thames & Hudson Inc., 500 Fifth Avenue, New York, New York 10110

British Library Cataloguing-in-Publication Data.
A catalogue record for this book is available from the British Library

Library of Congress Control Number 2022937730

ISBN 978-0-500-65317-3

Printed in China

Be the first to know about our new releases,
exclusive content and author events by visiting
**thamesandhudson.com**
**thamesandhudsonusa.com**
**thamesandhudson.com.au**